KU-040-006

ONE

WORLD

AT A

TIME

TED KOOSER

ONE WORLD AT A TIME

UNIVERSITY OF PITTSBURGH PRESS

Published by the University of Pittsburgh Press, Pittsburgh, Pa. 15260
Copyright © 1985, Ted Kooser
All rights reserved
Feffer and Simons, Inc., London
Manufactured in the United States of America


Library of Congress Cataloging in Publication Data

Kooser, Ted.
    One world at a time.

    (Pitt poetry series)
    I. Title.  II. Series.
PS3561.0606    1985        811'.54        84-19636
ISBN 0-8229-3504-X
ISBN 0-8229-5366-8 (pbk.)

"A Monday in May" originally appeared in *The Agni Review*. "In the Basement of the Goodwill Store" and "Walking at Noon Near the Burlington Depot in Lincoln, Nebraska" were first published in *The Black Warrior Review*. "The Carousel Goat in the Circus Museum" originally appeared in *The Chowder Review*. "A Roadside Shrine in Kansas" and "Latvian Neighborhood" are reprinted from *Columbia*. "A Letter" was originally published in *Cutbank*. "A Quarter Moon Just Before Dawn" and "An Empty Shotgun Shell" first appeared in *Field*. "Just Now" is reprinted from *The Georgia Review*. "A Room in the Past," "A Sunset," "Central," "The Giant Slide," "The Pitch," and "The Onion Woman" were originally published in *The Greenfield Review*. "The Ride" originally appeared in *MSS*. "A Patch of Sunlight," "Cleaning a Bass," and "Myrtle" were first published in *Nebraska Review*. "An August Night" is reprinted from *The New Jersey Poetry Journal*. "Daddy Longlegs" first appeared in *New Letters*. The poem "The Fan in the Window" appeared originally in *The New Yorker*. "A Child's Grave Marker," "Hobo Jungle," "In January, 1962," and "Porch Swing in September" are reprinted from *Pendragon*. "A Buffalo Skull," "A Fencerow in Early March," "At the Center," "At Midnight," "At Nightfall," "Camera," "Carp," and "Ladder" were originally published in *Plainsong*. "A Birthday Card," "The Mouse," "The Sigh," "The Urine Specimen," and "The Witness" originally appeared in *Poetry*. "Good-bye" and "The Voyager II Satellite" were first published in *Poetry Now*. "As the President Spoke," "Father," and "Flying at Night" are reprinted from *Prairie Schooner*. "Laundry" first appeared in *The Sandhills*. "At the Office Early" is reprinted from *Southern Poetry Review*. "Decoration Day" was originally published in *The Windflower Home Almanac of Poetry*.

A number of the poems in this book were written with the encouragement of a Creative Writing Fellowship from the National Endowment for the Arts.

*The publication of this book is supported by grants from the National Endowment for the Arts in Washington, D.C., a Federal agency, and the Pennsylvania Council on the Arts.*

*for Leonard Nathan*

# CONTENTS

# CONTENTS

# FLYING AT NIGHT

Above us, stars. Beneath us, constellations.
Five billion miles away, a galaxy dies
like a snowflake falling on water. Below us,
some farmer, feeling the chill of that distant death,
snaps on his yard light, drawing his sheds and barn
back into the little system of his care.
All night, the cities, like shimmering novas,
tug with bright streets at lonely lights like his.

# A FENCEROW IN EARLY MARCH

The last snowdrifts
have drawn themselves up
out of the light,
clinging to winter.
Beyond them,
a muddy stubble field
has sponged up
all the darkness—
the February nights,
the iron stoves,
the ink of every letter
written in longing.
And the fencerow
goes on, up and over
the next low rise
and the next, casting
a cold, white shadow,
each gate still closed
to spring.

# JUST NOW

Just now, if I look back down
the cool street of the past, I can see
streetlamps, one for each year,
lighting small circles of time
into which someone will step
if I squint, if I try hard enough—
circles smaller and smaller,
leading back to the one faint point
at the start, like a star.
So many of them are empty now,
those circles of roadside and grass.
In one, the moth of some feeling
still flutters, unspoken,
the cold darkness around it enormous.

# A BIRTHDAY CARD

In her eighties now, and weak and ill
with emphysema, my aunt sends me
a birthday card—a tossing ocean
with clipper ship—and wishes me
well at forty-four. She's included
a note—hard-bitten in ball-point,
with a pen that sometimes skips whole words
but never turns back—to tell me
her end of the news: how the steroids
have softened her spine, and now how
every x-ray shows more shattered bone.
Her hasty words skip in and out,
their little grooves washed clean of ink,
the message rising and falling
like short-wave radio, sending
this hurried SOS, with love.

# IN THE BASEMENT
# OF THE GOODWILL STORE

In musty light, in the thin brown air
of damp carpet, doll heads and rust,
beneath long rows of sharp footfalls
like nails in a lid, an old man stands
trying on glasses, lifting each pair
from the box like a glittering fish
and holding it up to the light
of a dirty bulb. Near him, a heap
of enameled pans as white as skulls
looms in the catacomb shadows,
and old toilets with dry red throats
cough up bouquets of curtain rods.

You've seen him somewhere before.
He's wearing the green leisure suit
you threw out with the garbage,
and the Christmas tie you hated,
and the ventilated wingtip shoes
you found in your father's closet
and wore as a joke. And the glasses
which finally fit him, through which
he looks to see you looking back—
two mirrors which flash and glance—
are those through which one day
you too will look down over the years,
when you have grown old and thin
and no longer particular,
and the things you once thought
you were rid of forever
have taken you back in their arms.

# CAMERA

It's an old box camera,
a Brownie, the color and shape
of the battery out of a car,
but smaller, lighter.
All the good times—
the clumsy picnics on the grass,
the new Dodge,
the Easter Sundays—
each with its own clear instant
in the fluid of time,
all these have leaked away,
leaving this shell,
this little battery without a spark.

# A ROOM IN THE PAST

It's a kitchen. Its curtains fill
with a morning light so bright
you can't see beyond its windows
into the afternoon. A kitchen
falling through time with its things
in their places, the dishes jingling
up in the cupboard, the bucket
of drinking water rippled as if
a truck had just gone past, but that truck
was thirty years. No one's at home
in this room. Its counter is wiped,
and the dishrag hangs from its nail,
a dry leaf. In housedresses of mist,
blue aprons of rain, my grandmother
moved through this life like a ghost,
and when she had finished her years,
she put them all back in their places
and wiped out the sink, turning her back
on the rest of us, forever.

# IN JANUARY, 1962

With his hat on the table before him,
my grandfather waited until it was time
to go to my grandmother's funeral.
Beyond the window, his eighty-eighth winter
lay white in its furrows. The little creek
which cut through his cornfield was frozen.
Past the creek and the broken, brown stubble,
on a hill which thirty years before
he'd given the town, a green tent flapped
under the cedars. Throughout the day before,
he'd stayed there by the window watching
the blue woodsmoke from the thawing-barrels
catch in the bitter wind and vanish,
and had seen, so small in the distance,
a man breaking the earth with a pick.
I suppose he could feel that faraway work
in his hands—the steel-smooth, cold oak handle;
the thick, dull shock at the wrists—
for the following morning, as we waited there,
it was as if it hurt him to move them,
those hard old hands which lay curled and still
near the soft gray felt hat on the table.

# TILLAGE MARKS

On this flat stone,
too heavy for one man alone
to pick up and carry
to the edge of his field,
are the faint white marks
of a plow, one plow
or many, the sharp blade
crisscrossing its face
like a lesson scratched there
in chalk, the same lesson
taught over and over,
to one man alone in his field
for fifty or sixty years,
or to fifty such men,
each alone, each plow striking
this stone, in this field
which he thought to be his.

# A CHILD'S GRAVE MARKER

A small block of granite
engraved with her name and the dates
just wasn't quite pretty enough
for this lost little girl
or her parents, who added a lamb
cast in plaster of paris,
using the same kind of cake mold
my grandmother had—iron,
heavy and black as a skillet.
The lamb came out coconut-white,
and seventy years have proven it
soft in the rain. On this hill,
overlooking a river in Iowa,
it melts in its own sweet time.

# FATHER

*Theodore Briggs Kooser*
*May 19, 1902–December 31, 1979*

You spent fifty-five years
walking the hard floors
of the retail business,
first, as a boy playing store

in your grandmother's barn,
sewing feathers on hats
that the neighbors threw out,
then stepping out onto

the smooth pine planks
of your uncle's grocery—
SALADA TEA in gold leaf
over the door, your uncle

and father still young then
in handlebar mustaches,
white aprons with dusters
tucked into their sashes—

then to the varnished oak
of a dry goods store—
music to your ears,
that bumpety-bump

of bolts of bright cloth
on the counter tops,
the small rattle of buttons,
the bell in the register—

then on to the cold tile
of a bigger store, and then one
still bigger—gray carpet,
wide aisles, a new town

**13**

to get used to—then into
retirement, a few sales
in your own garage,
the concrete under your feet.

You had good legs, Dad,
and a good storekeeper's eye:
asked once if you remembered
a teacher of mine,

you said, "I certainly do;
size ten, a little something
in blue." How you loved
what you'd done with your life!

Now you're gone, and the clerks
are lazy, the glass cases
smudged, the sale sweaters
pulled off on the floor.

But what good times we had
before it was over:
after those stores had closed,
you posing as customers,

strutting in big flowered hats,
those aisles like a stage,
the pale manikins watching;
we laughed till we cried.

# AT MIDNIGHT

Somewhere in the night,
a dog is barking,
starlight like beads of dew
along his tight chain.
No one is there
beyond the dark garden,
nothing to bark at
except, perhaps, the thoughts
of some old man
sending his memories
out for a midnight walk,
a rich cape
woven of many loves
swept recklessly
about his shoulders.

# CENTRAL

As fine a piece of furniture
as any Steinway, all oak
and nickel and Bakelite,
her switchboard stood in the kitchen
stretching the truth. While she sat
with her ear to the valley,
rumor reached its red tendrils
from socket to socket, from farm
to farm. When the sun went down,
she sat in the dark. Those voices
she'd listened to all afternoon,
clear as the high sharp cries of geese,
flew over the house and were gone.
The loose lines buzzed. In the moonlight,
her hands held the wilted bouquets
of pink rubber. "Central," she'd say
to the darkness, "This is Central.
Hello? Is there anyone there?"

# THE FAN IN THE WINDOW

It is September, and a cool breeze
from somewhere ahead is turning the blades;
night, and the slow flash of the fan
the last light between us and the darkness.
Dust has begun to collect on the blades,
haymaker's dust from distant fields,
dust riding to town on the night-black wings
of the crows, a thin frost of dust
which clings to the fan in just the way
we cling to the earth as it spins.
The fan has brought us through,
its shiny blades like the screw of a ship
that has pushed its way through summer—
cut flowers awash in its wake,
the stagnant Sargasso Sea of July
far behind us. For the moment, we rest,
we lie in the dark hull of the house,
we rock in the troughs off the shore
of October, the engine cooling,
the fan blades so lazily turning, but turning.

# MYRTLE

Wearing her yellow rubber slicker,
Myrtle, our *Journal* carrier,
has come early through rain and darkness
to bring us the news.
A woman of thirty or so,
with three small children at home,
she's told me she likes
a long walk by herself in the morning.
And with pride in her work,
she's wrapped the news neatly in plastic—
a bread bag, beaded with rain,
that reads WONDER.
From my doorway I watch her
flicker from porch to porch as she goes,
a yellow candle flame
no wind or weather dare extinguish.

# DADDY LONGLEGS

Here, on fine long legs springy as steel,
a life rides, sealed in a small brown pill
that skims along over the basement floor
wrapped up in a simple obsession.
Eight legs reach out like the master ribs
of a web in which some thought is caught
dead center in its own small world,
a thought so far from the touch of things
that we can only guess at it. If mine,
it would be the secret dream
of walking alone across the floor of my life
with an easy grace, and with love enough
to live on at the center of myself.

# GOOD-BYE

You lean with one arm out
against the porch post,
your big hand cupping its curve,
shy of that handshake
we both know is coming.
And when we've said enough,
when the last small promises
begin to repeat, your eyes
come to mine, and then
you offer your hand,
dusted with chalk from the post,
and sticky with parting.

II

# THE GIANT SLIDE

Beside the highway, the Giant Slide
with its rusty undulations lifts
out of the weeds. It hasn't been used
for a generation. The ticket booth
tilts to that side where the nickels shifted
over the years. A chain link fence keeps out
the children and drunks. Blue morning glories
climb halfway up the stairs, bright clusters
of laughter. Call it a passing fancy,
this slide that nobody slides down now.
Those screams have all gone east
on a wind that will never stop blowing
down from the Rockies and over the plains,
where things catch on for a little while,
bright leaves in a fence, and then are gone.

# A ROADSIDE SHRINE IN KANSAS

Sunk into the earth
end up,
as if it had fallen
white as a comet
from heaven,
this bathtub,
clenching its claws
into fists,
now shelters
a Virgin
of plaster,
while through
the rusty drain hole,
one kneeling there
can see
in the shimmering distance,
God
walking the bean rows.

# DECORATION DAY

It takes the hard work
of a dozen ants
to open each bud
of a peony.
For weeks, there they are,
clickety-clack,
biting the sutures
and licking the glue.
Then, one by one
on Decoration Day,
the blossoms explode,
tossing the ants
all over the yard.
Early that morning,
we find these flowers
opened, pink and white,
and in the wet grass,
hundreds of ants
with the staggers, all
watching the sky.

# A MONDAY IN MAY

It rained all weekend,
but today the peaked roofs
are as dusty and warm
as the backs of old donkeys
tied in the sun.
So much alike are our houses,
our lives. Under every eave—
leaf, cobweb, and feather;
and for each front yard
one sentimental maple,
who after a shower has passed,
weeps into her shadow
for hours.

# A BUFFALO SKULL

No fine white bone-sheen now;
a hundred hard years
have worn it away, this stump
washed up on a bar
in the river, its horns
like broken roots,
its muzzle filled with sand
and the thin gray breath
of spider webs. Once,
they covered the grasslands
like the shadows of clouds,
and now the river gives up
just one skull, a hive of bone
like a fallen wasp's nest,
heavy, empty, and
full of the whine of the wind
and old thunder.

# LAUNDRY

A pink house trailer,
scuffed and rusted, sunken
in weeds. On the line,

five pale blue workshirts
up to their elbows
in raspberry canes—

a good, clean crew
of pickers, out early,
sleeves wet with dew,

and near them, a pair
of bright yellow panties
urging them on.

# THE MOUSE

On the floor of a parking garage
I found a dead mouse. It was winter,
the world gone gray outside and in,
and the mouse a part of all that drabness—
the smallest part. He stood
like a windup mouse run down at last
but still on its wheels, a fast run
just behind him, and he'd pulled
his paws up tightly under his chin
as if he'd stopped to sniff at the edge
of something important—a mousehole maybe,
right under his nose and opening
out of the world. His back was arched
against entering there, and every muscle
had frozen in place like a spring.

# LADDER

Against the low roof of a house
in the suburbs, someone has left
a ladder leaning, an old wooden ladder
too heavy to take down at night
and put up in the morning, the kind
that reaches beyond such a roof
by a good six feet, punching up
into the sky. The kind with paint
from another world on its rungs,
the cream and butter colored spots
from another time, the kind that
before you get up in the morning
knocks hard at the front of your house
like a sheriff, that stands there
in front of your door with a smile;
a ladder with solid authority,
with its pantlegs pressed, a ladder
that if it could whistle would whistle.

# WALKING AT NOON NEAR THE
# BURLINGTON DEPOT
# IN LINCOLN, NEBRASKA

*to the memory of James Wright*

On the rat-gray dock
of the candy factory,
workers in caps and aprons
as white as divinity
sit on their heels and smoke
in the warm spring sunlight
thick with butterscotch.

In the next block down,
outside a warehouse,
its big doors rolled and bolted
over the dusty hush
of pyramids of cartons,
two pickets in lettered vests
call back and forth, their voices
a clatter of echoes.

A girl sits in her car,
an old tan Oldsmobile
broken down over its tires,
and plays the radio.

On the grill of a semi
smelling of heat and distance,
one tattered butterfly.

And an empty grocery cart
from Safeway, miles from here,
leans into its reflection
in a blackened window, a little
piano recital of chrome
for someone to whom all things
were full of sadness.

# A PATCH OF SUNLIGHT

Over the old dog's eye,
the blue cloud
of a cataract.
Along one leg, a tremor—
some tiny animal
running in long brown grass.

# CARP

On the river bottom,
the carp have blown out
all the candles.

They whisper along
over the closed, black
bibles of clams.

Water-monks these,
with mouths like those
of angels singing,

but not angelic,
so very naked now
in darkness,

their cool, hard bodies
touching, among
the tapestries of weed.

# AT THE CENTER

In Kansas, on top
of an old piano,
a starfish, dry
as a fancy pastry
left sitting there
during a wedding,
spreads its brown arms
over the foam
of a white lace doily,
reaching for water
in five directions.

# A SUNSET

The steeple so carefully
swings its long shadow
over the grass that the bell's
small shadow does not ring,
nor do the soft gray shadows
of its pigeons fly. Light
rises into the treetops
like the bubbles in beer.
A man walks home alone,
his shadow, shambling ahead,
some dark old woman
who rents out rooms.
She's wrapped in a shawl
that hides her face
in folds of blackness,
and closed in her fist
is the evening star.

# THE RIDE

*to the memory of John Gardner*

High in the night, we rock, we rock in the stars
while the Ferris wheel stops to let someone off
in the darkness below, someone we saw there
a half turn ahead of us, riding alone,
a man with white hair who threw up his hands
going down. We were too frightened for that.
We held on with both hands as we followed him,
climbing and falling, around and around,
while the world turned beneath us, rolled under
the wheel with its music, its flickering lights.
Now we rock in the starlight. Beneath us,
the music has stopped, the motor pops at idle.
The midway goes dark, booth to booth, as he passes.

# AT NIGHTFALL

In feathers the color of dusk, a swallow,
up under the shadowy eaves of the barn,
weaves now, with skillful beak and chitter,
one bright white feather into her nest
to guide her flight home in the darkness.
It has taken a hundred thousand years
for a bird to learn this one trick with a feather,
a simple thing. And the world is alive
with such innocent progress. But to what
safe place shall any of us return
in the last smoky nightfall,
when we in our madness have put the torch
to the hope in every nest and feather?

# AT THE OFFICE EARLY

Rain has beaded the panes
of my office windows,
and in each little lens
the bank at the corner
hangs upside down.
What wonderful music
this rain must have made
in the night, a thousand banks
turned over, the change
crashing out of the drawers
and bouncing upstairs
to the roof, the soft
percussion of ferns
dropping out of their pots,
the ball-point pens
popping out of their sockets
in a fluffy snow
of deposit slips.
Now all day long,
as the sun dries the glass,
I'll hear the soft piano
of banks righting themselves,
the underpaid tellers
counting their nickels and dimes.

# CLEANING A BASS

She put it on the chopping block
and it flopped a little, the red rick-rack
of its sharp gills sawing the evening air
into lengths, its yellow eyes like glass,
like the eyes of a long-forgotten doll
in the light of an attic. "They feel no pain,"
she told me, setting the fish upright,
and with a chunk of stovewood
she drove an ice pick through its skull
and into the block. The big fish curled
on its pin like a silver pennant
and then relaxed, but I could see life
in those eyes, which stared at the darkening
world of the air with a terrible wonder.
"It's true," she said, looking over at me
through the gathering shadows, "they feel no pain,"
and she took her Swedish filleting knife
with its beautiful blade that leaped and flashed
like a fish itself, and with one stroke
laid the bass bare to its shivering spine.

# AN EMPTY SHOTGUN SHELL

It's a handsome thing
in its uniform—
all crimson and brass—
standing guard
at the gate to the field,
but something
is wrong at its heart.
It's dark in there,
so dark a whole night
could squeeze in,
could shrink back up in there
like a spider,
a black one
with smoke in its hair.

# A QUARTER MOON JUST BEFORE DAWN

There's sun on the moon's back
as she stoops to pick up
a star that she's dropped in her garden.
And stars keep falling,
through little holes in the bottoms
of her sweater pockets.
She's stretched them out
by hiding her hands all these years—
big peasant's hands
with night under their nails.

# A LETTER

I have tried a dozen ways
to say those things
and have failed: how the moon
with its bruises
climbs branch over branch
through the empty tree;
how the cool November dusk,
like a wind, has blown
these old gray houses up
against the darkness;
and what these things
have come to mean to me
without you. I raked the yard
this morning, and it rained
this afternoon. Tonight,
along the shiny street,
the bags of leaves—
wet-shouldered
but warm in their skins—
are huddled together, close
so close to life.

# LATVIAN NEIGHBORHOOD

Along this street,
snow blows
from the shoulders
of old houses,
lifts,
catches the wind
like long white hair,
like pipe smoke,
like the thin gray scarves
of immigrants
standing in line,
hands in their pockets,
cold fingers
pinching the lint
of their stories.

# THE VOYAGER II SATELLITE

The tin man is cold;
the glitter of distant worlds
is like snow on his coat.
Free-falling through space,
he spreads his arms
and slowly turns,
hands reaching to catch
the white, elusive
dandelion fuzz
of starlight. He is the dove
with wings of purest gold
sent out upon the deep
to seek a place for us,
the goat upon whose back
we've sent out problems
into exile, the dreamy beast
of peace and science
who now grows smaller, smaller,
falling so gracefully
into the great blank face
of God.

# THE CAROUSEL GOAT
# IN THE CIRCUS MUSEUM

No pony who smartly lifts one hoof
to the gay calliope, or swan
who floats like an open water lily
round and around; no loping white hare
whose ears fold smoothly over his back
like the finest gloves, oh, no; not he—
nothing so pretty as that. This goat
is goat foremost, with a skull like stone
from which his eyes like flies in amber
peer at the circling world. The skin
of his horns has peeled and burst
like some horrible fruit, and his tongue
is red and swollen, lolling out
over his yellow teeth. Though he wears
a baby-blue saddle, it doesn't help.
He's a filthy beast of the fields
and he looks the part. In my dreams,
I have ridden him round in dusty circles
in pursuit of the girl on the swan,
and have felt the harsh laughter beneath me
as I clutched his hard spine through the night.

# THE WITNESS

The divorce judge has asked for a witness,
and you wait at the back of the courtroom
as still as a flag on its stand, your best dress
falling in smooth, even folds that begin now
to gather the dust of white bouquets
which like a veil of lace is lifting
away from the kiss of the sunlit windows.

In your lap, where you left them, your hands
lie fallen apart like the rinds of a fruit.
Whatever they cupped has been eaten away.
Beyond you, across a lake of light
where years have sunk and settled to the floor,
the voices drone on with the hollow sound
of boats rubbing a dock that they're tied to.

You know what to say when they call you.

# AS THE PRESIDENT SPOKE

As the President spoke, he raised a finger
to emphasize something he said. I've forgotten
just what he was saying, but as he spoke
he glanced at that finger as if it were
somebody else's, and his face went slack and gray,
and he folded his finger back into his hand
and put it down under the podium
along with whatever it meant, with whatever he'd seen
as it spun out and away from that bony axis.

# THE PITCH

Tight on the fat man's wrist
is a watch with a misty face.
His hand is hot on your sleeve.
He wants you to give him a minute,

friend, of your precious time.
He's got something for you
and the little lady. Call it
security, call it insurance,

call it aluminum siding.
Subscribe to these six magazines,
and the fat man wins a nice trip
to Hawaii, friend, a nice trip

to Acapulco. A fat man
hasn't much time in this world.
His pulse has one foot in a cast.
On his cheeks, red cobwebs appear.

He's got the Moose Lodge on his breath
like a vinegar bath, and his eyes
are yellow caution lights. Listen,
he's got a little woman, *too.*

# THE SIGH

You lie in your bed and sigh,
and the springs deep in the mattress
sing out with the same low note,
mocking your sadness. It's hard—
not the mattress, but life.
Life is hard. All along
you thought you could trust in
your own bed, your own sorrow.
You thought you were sleeping alone.

# THE ONION WOMAN

All of the clothes she owns
she wears in layers, coat
upon coat upon coat
like an onion. She's wrapped
the woman inside, the taste
of the woman, her odors,
her heart. But the fear
still shows through all those skins—
that tight white core
where the shoot has withered.

# HOBO JUNGLE

A fat brown car seat, mushy with rain.
A few fire-blackened cans. A bucket
without any bottom but holding
a full measure of cottonwood leaves.
Not much of a story. You've heard it all
time and again—a few rusty words
enclosing a center of darkness, an edge
that can cut if you try prying the lid.

# AN AUGUST NIGHT

High in the trees, cicadas weave
a wickerwork of longing.
In the shadows between two houses,
a man peers into a room
through the hum of a window fan,
the fragrance of his hair oil
like distant music, far too faint
to awaken the naked girl
on the clean linen of moonlight.

# THE URINE SPECIMEN

In the clinic, a sun-bleached shell of stone
on the shore of the city, you enter
the last small chamber, a little closet
chastened with pearl—cool, white, and glistening,
and over the chilly well of the toilet
you trickle your precious sum in a cup.
It's as simple as that. But the heat
of this gold your body's melted and poured out
into a form begins to enthrall you,
warming your hand with your flesh's fevers
in a terrible way. It's like holding
an organ—spleen or fatty pancreas,
a lobe from your foamy brain still steaming
with worry. You know that just outside
a nurse is waiting to cool it into a gel
and slice it onto a microscope slide
for the doctor, who in it will read your future,
wringing his hands. You lift the chalice and toast
the long life of your friend there in the mirror,
who wanly smiles, but does not drink to you.

# THE HEART PATIENT

He lowers his voice when he mentions it,
the way one speaks of someone
seated at a nearby table: Don't look now,
but when you get an opportunity, see?
There is that stranger, my heart.

And later, after the talk has come round
to something to laugh at,
I steal a quick look at his chest—
the white shirt, the blue paisley tie—
beneath which I see what he means:

a man seated alone in an all-night café,
drumming his fingers,
a blank look on his face
as he watches the doorway, the darkness
beyond the dead ferns in the window.

# GERONIMO'S MIRROR

That flash from a distant hillside,
that firefly in the blue shadows of rock—
that's Geronimo's mirror.
After all of these years, he's up there
still trying to warn us
that the soldiers are coming.
He sees them riding along the horizon
in an endless line,
sees them dipping down into the valley
rider by rider.
His mirror or tin, cupped in his palm,
says they're nearer now.
It says he can hear the black rock
sounding under their hooves,
can smell the sharp smoke of dust in the air.
Now he can hear their dark voices,
the old voices of horses,
and the talk that is leather's.
And now they are climbing the hill,
that holy hill that is Geronimo's,
but he is not afraid.
His mirror is warning the others,
and we are the others.

# PORCH SWING IN SEPTEMBER

The porch swing hangs fixed in a morning sun
that bleaches its gray slats, its flowered cushion
whose flowers have faded, like those of summer,
and a small brown spider has hung out her web
on a line between porch post and chain
so that no one may swing without breaking it.
She is saying it's time that the swinging were done with,
time that the creaking and pinging and popping
that sang through the ceiling were past,
time now for the soft vibrations of moths,
the wasp tapping each board for an entrance,
the cool dewdrops to brush from her work
every morning, one world at a time.

## PITT POETRY SERIES

**Ed Ochester, General Editor**